THE HYDROPONIC GARDEN

A START UP GUIDE TO A FLOURISHING AND ABUNDANT HYDROPONIC YIELD
HYDROPONICS FOR BEGINNERS

BETTER GARDENING GUIDES

COPYRIGHT

DISCLAIMER

Kindle 5 Star Books

Free Kindle 5 Star Book Club Membership

Join Other Kindle 5 Star Members Who Are Getting Private Access To Weekly Free Kindle Book Promotions

Get free Kindle books

Stay connected:

Join our Facebook group

Follow Kindle 5 Star on Twitter

Also, if you want to receive updates on Better Gardening Guide's new books, free promotions and Kindle countdown deals sign up to their New Release Mailing List.

TABLE OF CONTENTS

INTRODUCTION

You love to garden and now you want to try something new! The advancements in how we garden has grown leaps and bounds over the years, and hydroponics is one of the key advancements that has helped gardening thrive through ancient times. It's easier than you think, and with some dedication your garden can flourish. Whether you want to grow vegetables for you and your family, or you want to create a beautiful herb garden, hydroponics is a way to expand your techniques and have a hand in an adventure with something new.

You can pick and choose from six different systems and setups. What you choose should be based on your preferred type, as well as the one best suited to your ideal growth. Over the next few chapters you will have an insight into these systems, as well as the key components that make each system thrive. The best part about it is that you don't have to be a professional. You can start at the very beginning and gain the knowledge you need to be successful. When you're finished, you will be ready and eager to take the steps to begin your own system.

There are also many advances in hydroponics. From the types of substrates, to the way to design your system everything about hydroponics has evolved. Individually, you will have to understand the time and cost involved no matter what type of system you use. If you want a simple garden, perhaps a drip or wick method is for you or perhaps, you want more than a few plants. If so, then the ebb and flow system may be your best option. Whatever you decide this book is an introduction to the basic principles and design of hydroponics, and a better understanding of how it works, why it works and what you can do to start one of your own.

The key to learning about hydroponics is to explore what works for you and the space allotted in your home or greenhouse. You can create a massive set up with a variety of plants, or keep it simple. The choice is yours. I suggest you consider what you're looking for and how many plants you are considering as you read on and gain a better understanding of each system's pros and cons. You can grow a plant or two and have a thriving business. It's all up to the green thumb in you!

CHAPTER 1

For years the premise about gardening in general is that it takes three things: water, sunlight and nutrient rich soil. Though gardening is simple, there are new and exciting developments that allow us to try our hand at something new. By definition hydroponics is the ability to grow plants without the use of a traditional dirt medium and instead using a water solution, which is rich in nutrients. Hydroponics explores the ideas that other things such as clay, Perlite, Vermiculite, Pro-Mix and Coconut Fiber can be used as a support system for your plants. There are several branches of hydroponics, which we will explore in detail later but typically they include;

- Wick

- Water Culture

- Ebb and Flow

- Drip

- N.F.T.

- Aeroponic.

Each one differs in set up, but all bring wonderful results that you can use. Though hydroponics is something that has taken on a new trend in society today. The earliest noted use of hydroponics was found in ancient Egyptian hieroglyphic records dating as far back as hundreds of years B.C. Throughout time hydroponics have shown up in other places as well. Some records show that the Chinese, as well as Mexican Aztecs, all have records of "floating gardens."

As you can see the use of hydroponics is nothing new, however, researchers have experimented with different types of hydroponic set ups and types of growth. Early in the research it was found that hydroponics were great for use in areas of the world that simply could not grow anything in soil. The set-up of a hydroponic system allowed them to still grow food they can eat, despite where they live. One of the most memorable uses of hydroponics was during WWII when troops used a hydroponic system to eat fresh produce because they were stationed in islands in the Pacific that would not grow these items in the ground.

Soon after, hydroponics became better known, and people were eager to try it out. Everyone from NASA to traditional farmers, to those people working on home gardens, began researching and exploring the idea of hydroponics and the benefits to using this type of system. The term hydroponics was actually first used in 1937 right at the beginning when it started to become more popular. One pioneer in hydroponic development was Sir Francis Bacon in the early 1600's. He had a great platform, but by using only distilled water his results did poorly. It wasn't until years later that studies showed that the micronutrients in normal water were essential to helping the plants grow vibrant and beautiful.

CHAPTER 2

The first step of your hydroponic system is to decide which setup is going to work for you. As mentioned before, there are six basic setups that will help you create your beautiful hydroponic garden at home. Each setup has its own set of benefits and varies in cost.

The first set up is called the Wick System. This system is by far the easiest of the six, and has the simplest of designs for someone starting out. The design is made up of a passive type system with no moving parts. Since the wick system uses this passive set up, it makes it not only cheaper to start, but it's also easy to maintain. The positives to these types of systems are many, but there are a few drawbacks as well.

Plants that require a lot of water, or thirsty plants, such as tomatoes do not do well in these types of systems. When you are using a wick system the ideal plants to grow are typically quick growing plants, such as herbs and lettuces. This is important to keep in mind when choosing a system based on what you plan to use it for.   The key factor of a wick system is that it uses more than one wick that will deliver the water to the roots of the plants, from the reservoir. The setup of a wick system typically is made up of four components; grow tray, wick, aeration and reservoir.

In order for you to really understand it's important that we define the terminology that will show up from time to time. A wick, by definition, is a cord or strand of loosely woven, twisted, or braided fibers, as a cotton rope, that draws up the liquid by capillary action. So now that we know what the wick is what is the capillary action exactly? This is the interaction between the liquid, in this case the nutrient rich water, and the solid, the rope the two meet and the liquid travels through the rope. This is how the liquid reaches the plant through the wick.

The growth tray with a wick system differs from all other setups in that it uses a growing medium to entirely fill up a tray, and not use net pots. The growth trays can be anything that you use which is moveable and contain the mess of your plants, such as the substrate or medium. The amount of medium used is one that drains slowly, allowing the full use of the capillary action. Each medium plays a key element in the support of your setup. Some of the most common mediums used are Perlite and Vermiculite. The reservoir with a wick system is basically the same as it is in any other hydroponic system. The reservoir is a large container containing fertilized water, which sits beneath the growth tray and feeds nutrients rich water to the plants.

Next we have the aeration for the system. Typically this is a common combination of a pump along with an air stone. You can often find air stones in the aquarium section of your local pet store. A plastic tube connects the two and air is pushed through the stone. This distributes oxygen through the water to the plants.

With a water culture system things are different. The water culture system works entirely on filling up a reservoir and allowing the roots of your plants to bathe in the nutrient rich solution, simultaneously using an air pump to flow oxygen to the plants as well. There is an ease of use with this type of system much like the wick system. There is only one piece of equipment to worry about, but you must pay close attention to your plants to avoid disaster. If there should be an issue with the air pump line, the plants can literally drown. The key in making this system work is to make sure your air pump is always working. It may be beneficial to invest in a more expensive, better quality air pump if you can, so that you can be rest assured your pump will always be performing at its best. Unlike the wick system, the water culture system uses netted pots. A netted pot is usually a small black pot with holes that allow for the free flow of water. As your plants grow, the nutrients in the water may need to be changed regularly as well.

The Ebb and Flow system is also known as the Flood and Drain system. Basically what this means is that there is a growth tray holding your pots filled with substrate of some kind. This could be clay pellets, wool or some other medium. There is a timer on the system that will begin regularly scheduled intervals, which will trigger the start the pump and fill the reservoir. The reservoir will fill until it can reach the roots of the plants and then drains the water back down when it is finished. The regularly set timers keep the roots of the plants sporadically covered in nutrients and air.

Today Ebb and Flow systems are typically found in home gardens for the beginner, also much like the wick system. There are a few drawbacks that make the ebb and flow system less desirable than other systems. The most notable is that the roots tend to grow together, which means more work for the owner. They can spend more time than they would like to remove and harvest damaged plants. When you have this problem the quality and yield from plants in these conditions are usually poor if not addressed. It can manifest in brown and yellow spots on the leaves as well.

The next type of system is the Drip system. The basic idea behind a drip system of hydroponics is a choice between a recovery or a non-recovery system. The drip system is also used widely in the world. The operation is easy, with the use of a timer in a submersed pump. The pump them pulls the nutrient rich water up and "drips" onto the plants using a drip line. A drip line is usually a tube with holes in it which allows the water to flow through it.   In a recovery system all of the runoff nutrients are run down and recollected into the reservoir. If you choose to use a non-recovery system the nutrient rich water is not collected and reused again.

My experience is that using a recovery system uses the water more efficiently by using the excess water continually. In addition, it allows for a less expensive timer since the timing controls aren't as specific as in some other setups. If you decided that a non-recovery system is more your style, a more advanced timer would be used because the water would need to be specifically adjusted to make sure the plants are getting as much nutrient rich water as they need. It's important to note that if you're using a recovery system, you have to be careful to check the nutrient level and be sure to keep it regulated as you reuse the water and drop it back onto the plants you're growing. On the opposing side of this if you're not reusing the water and are using a non-recovery system you can fill the reservoir full of pH balanced nutrient water and let it go, not having to pay close attention to the balance of nutrients since once used it will be run off anyway.

N. F. T. or Nutrient Film Technique hydroponic systems are what typically comes to mind for most people when someone asks them about hydroponics. Don't let the name scare you. This type of hydroponics has a consistent flow of nutrients and there is timer necessary for the system to work properly. The nutrients are led into the grow tray through a line pulling the flow up and into the tray and running over the roots of the plants. With this type of system, there is typically no medium used. This is especially important for someone who wants to eliminate the need for those materials, and the time and energy spent setting them up. Think of a mesh screen across the tank and allowing the roots to dangle through them. This will keep the water flowing freely over the hanging roots. The biggest culprit for this system is some type of mechanical failure. If the pump stops working, perhaps due to a loss of power, the roots will get no flow of nutrients. If the system is shifted or moved somehow, it won't allow for the nutrients to flow as they are intended and cause the same outcome. It's important to make sure your setup is accurate in dimensions so that your roots are fed thoroughly and not dried out. This type of system is often what teachers use in classrooms today. This allows for students to see the roots of the plants they are growing and will keep them interested!

The last type of hydroponics is the most challenging and what most people consider to be the "high tech" of hydroponics. Much like the NFT system above this design allows the roots of the plants to be exposed without a medium. The thing that sets Aeroponics apart from other systems is how the plants are arranged. Each plant is suspended in the air in this system design. The plants are then are misted with nutrient rich water. This type of system is more involved because of the necessary use of a timer and the specific settings needed to make sure your plants don't dry out. The mist is usually sprayed every few minutes, keeping the roots of the plants fed and moist. The specifics of the Aeroponics approach really leads it to be in a class of its own. It uses no growth medium and is not using a flow of water, which sets it apart from the other systems. Since it does, however, use water in the spray, it's important to include it in this list because most consider it a form of hydroponics.

We have discussed the setups of each system and the components, but we haven't specifically addressed what exactly nutrient rich water is. As I mentioned before Sir Bacon thought that by using distilled water and stripping it of minerals he was giving his plants the best chance for growth. Today, when we are creating the nutrient rich water we have a much easier way of mixing the nutrients in the water in the reservoirs. Often it can be overwhelming when you start to research the types of nutrients you need to use. I suggest a "complete" nutrient solution that you can add to the water, which will work to feed the plants and keep them healthy. In nature, plants typically get their nutrients in decomposing leaves and organic matter. With hydroponics we instead deliver the fertilization in the water component of the set up.

CHAPTER 3

So we have covered the history and we have touched on the types of hydroponic systems. Now we need to understand what makes hydroponics work and what other things make up the tools for success. This chapter is all about substrates or medium. The best way to describe what a substrate is, in my opinion, is to think of a butterfly. Each wing of the butterfly is delicate and moveable. The thing that keeps each wing together is the center, or the body of the butterfly. When we use hydroponics we are eliminating our potting soil, thus losing the part of the plant holding it all together, the base. In hydroponics substrates are the things we can use to hold our plants where we want them. The main function of a substrate is support and mechanical in nature. Unlike soil the substrate plays no part in helping the water reach the roots. This is what makes a substrate only there in a supporting role. It's important to note all substrates are different and some do hold water. This can be useful in some systems that may need help if a part of the process isn't working correctly.

If you start your hydroponic garden and are looking for a simple answer to finding a substrate you will likely not get one. There are a number of types of substrates and combinations. For now, I will go over the most commonly used ones and explore their differences. The types of substrates you will typically find are clay granules, rock wool, perlite and vermiculite. You can also use sand, gravel or even packing peanuts. Each one of these is used in specific ways for different types of systems. If you use a good substrate they can retain the moisture and aerate the roots of your plants. This will help you to produce better quality growth and yield. Another term interchangeable for a substrate is a medium.

Clay granules are typically used in plants on a patio or in the home. They almost resemble little popcorn and are light weight. The fact that they are extremely porous makes it easy to use and are typically cheaper to buy. They come in pellet or pebble form and can be found at any local home store. Rock Wool is a substrate you will see used many times in hydroponics. Sometimes if you can't find rock wool you can look for slag or mineral wool. All of these are similar. The process of creating rock wool is one that is very interesting. Rock, or slag is heated to a staggering 1400 degrees C. Then, it's spun, much like cotton candy. These spun threads are mixed with a binding agent and create something that looks a lot like the insulation in your attic.

There are a number of pros and cons for using rock wool. The most important thing that will attract you to it is the fact that it holds and retains a lot of water. This can be a big help if something happens to your pump and you need time to replace it! A few other pros are that it's easy to use, easy to find, and holds enough air to keep the root aerated as well. The cons are also important. Rock Wool, though a wonderful substrate does not dispose of well. It is hard to get rid of and doesn't break down. Additionally, the dust fibers can be bad for your health and aren't very good for your lungs.

Perlite and Vermiculite have many commonalities with very few differences. It's important to understand them both as they have different parts to play in your hydroponic system. Both of these are volcanic rock, which is heated until it becomes a very light glass stone. The benefit to using Perlite is that it holds very little water, but has an abundance of air. It is often not used in systems where there is a flow of water because it is so light that it frequently can run along with the water and leave your plants exposed. Vermiculite is the opposite counterpart for Perlite. This particular substrate holds more water and less air and is a little heavier. Often time people use a mix of the two, especially if there is not enough of air or water. It can be used together to find an accurate combination to suit your needs.

One of the most commonly used, and simple to find substrate, is gravel. Gravel can frequently be found in the ebb and flow system because of its weight and durability. With that benefit, however, is also what makes it problematic. Gravel can be difficult to carry around because it's heavy and can damage plants if you're not careful. Another pitfall is that gravel is not porous at all and retains no water. You can't count on it if you have a power outage so be sure if you should choose gravel that you watch the water nutrient levels and be sure that your plants are not drying out.

Whichever substrate you use, be sure it's well suited to the time and effort you can put into your system. Hydroponics takes time and care, and the balance is the key factor in keeping your garden healthy and happy. As you plan out your hydroponic system, be sure to check each substrate composition and compare it to the types of plants you want to grow. Some substrates will not always work for each system or each type of plant. Be sure to know which substrate you are going to use before you buy your plants. Some common substrates can be cheap and readily available, while others may be harder to find. Keep that in mind as you move ahead!

CHAPTER 4

So we have discussed the systems, the substrate and the history, but what is pH exactly and why is it important? Let's start with the basics. PH is the potential hydrogen-hydroxyl ion content. To make it easier, let's think about a scale where you are weighing two items. One side you have some acidic juice and on the other you have some bread or your base. Much like the scale, when we use the pH in hydroponics it's important that the scale is weighed equally by both. Often overlooked, understanding and checking the pH level has a huge impact on the product you will grow.

Water has an equal balance of both hydrogen and hydroxyl and therefore has a neutral pH level of 7. Each level of pH in a solution multiplies as it increases. If the pH level in your solution is 4.0 then it contains ten times more acid than something where the pH level is 3.0 and so on. Based on your plants, what this means is if your pH level needs to be 6.0 to 7.0 you would have to adjust the pH level ten times more than the current level. I know it sounds complicated, but trust me, it's something that is good to know if you want to create a wonderful hydroponic system. Each type of plant will need a different pH level and it's nice to have a reference for it. Here are some of the common plant pH levels you may need to know in the future:

PLANT	PH RANGE TO USE
CABBAGE	6.5-7.5
CUCUMBERS	5.9-6.1
LETTUCE	6.0-6.5
PUMPKIN	5.1-6.6
RADISH	6.0-7.0
STRAWBERRIES	5.5-6.5
TOMATOES	5.5-6.5

When you need to check or adjust your pH it is fairly simple and there are several ways to do so. Typically the best way to check your pH level is to purchase paper test strips, which have a dye and allow you to compare the color of your water with the levels they show you. The only issues with this are that often the color differences can be hard to distinguish between. Another way to check your pH levels would be to purchase a liquid pH test kit. With this test, you add a slight amount of dye to a water sample. Similar in using the test strips this way is more accurate to read and often gives better results. Lastly, if you're a hardcore gardener, you can purchase a digital pH meter. Obviously the most accurate, they can come in big pieces of equipment or in something as small as a pen. Either way you use an electrode to test the sample water and are given the results. Find the right supplies for what you're doing and be sure to have some on hand whenever you need to test the pH levels in your hydroponic garden.

So now you've checked the pH level but how do you adjust it? The easiest and most effective things to have on hand are phosphoric acid (to decrease your pH) and potassium hydroxide, (to increase your pH). These are relatively harmless things you can easily buy and keep on hand. If you're not comfortable using them you can buy pH adjusters at local stores where everything has been mixed and is ready to go. The only issues with these are that they often cause huge shifts in the pH level and are harder to control. Adjust the pH level in your system slowly and be sure to check it regularly, and more often, after a change has been made to be sure the pH level is doing what you want it to. Over time you will develop a system that works for you and will have no issues adjusting the pH level next time. Don't be alarmed if the pH levels go up over time this is normal just be sure to check it with some regularity.

Now that pH is under control let's talk a little more nutrients. Nutrients are fertilizers that are added to the water, which are typically found in soil. As I mentioned before most fertilizers are found in nature. For hydroponics you can use extremely concentrated formulas, which have to be diluted. Often you can find fertilizers in both powder and liquid form and over time you can discover which type works best for you. Almost all fertilizers have no pH buffer so be sure to test the pH levels regularly. Much like soil, when someone is using hydroponics you can use organic or non-organic fertilizer. If you decided to use an organic system, it is much more difficult than if you don't. Sometimes organic particles compound and create issues with the pumps, often clogging them and causing issues with the system. Creating and maintaining your nutrient mix is something that needs to be individual based on your plants, as well as your system set up.

Chapter 5

Your head is full of information and you have taken a lot of notes down by now, but this is where the fun begins. If you look over the earlier chapters you can skip along until you find the basic set up instructions for the type of system you plan to create. Whatever you choose can be changed later, but for now stick with what you think you can handle.

- Wick System Set Up-

What to do:

1. Take your plant, rinse the roots free of the soil it was in, and place in a netted pot.

2. Gently fill the pot with your choice of substrate being careful to care for the roots.

3. Find and position a reservoir. This can be anything you choose such as a tub, or a large bucket.

4. Fill and mix your nutrient rich water using the fertilizer with the levels required for your particular type of plant.

5. Positon your wick, such as cotton rope. Run one end of the wick in the water and up along the side. Place the other end of the wick within the bottom half of your plant in the substrate.

- Water Culture Set Up-

1. Use an airtight container such as an aquarium and fill with nutrient water solution. Create a shield for the top of the aquarium to keep the light off of the water.

2. Use something to create a platform such as Styrofoam to use as a growth tray. Cut to fit on the top the reservoir with holes cut out for each plant.

3. Put your plants in netted pots filled with substrate. Slip each pot into one of the holes in your grow tray with the roots hanging down into the Styrofoam openings.

4. Assemble the air stone and pump. Run the air stone into the bottom of the tank and turn it on.

- Ebb and Flow Set Up-

   1. For this set up I am going to recommend you research kits that are available to you with a setup guide. This makes it much easier for you, the gardener, and allows you to have something concrete and easy to use. Typically when you purchase kits for this you can find some illustrations, which can help with this type of two pump system.

   I can tell you that some sites have specific ways of designing your system. A quick google search of Ebb and Flow can give you some vendors of this kit set up.

- Drip System Set Up-

      1. Put a reservoir in place. Assemble and place your growth tray over the reservoir with a drain hole directly above the reservoir.

      2. Fill your reservoir with a water nutrient solution based on your plant.

      3. Assemble and place your air pump with one tube directly connected to the air stone and the other leading up to the drip sector.

      4. Set up your drip system so that it is hanging over the plants with the spouts over each plant.

5. Finally, place your plants into a substrate in each cup and turn on the air stone.

- N.F.T System Set-Up

    1. Place your reservoir where you want your system to be.

    2. Place a growth tray with holes for the plants on top of the reservoir. Angle the growth tray so that one end is higher. The other end needs to be short enough so that water can flow down the growth tray and back into the reservoir. So make the lower end of the growth tray shorter.

    3. Find mesh screening and arrange your plants with the roots dangling through, no medium is necessary. Place them in the growth tray.

    4. Place your air stone into the reservoir, on the side where the growth tray is shorter. Run the line to the pump on the outside.

    5. Install a water pump, with a line, in the reservoir at the opposite side of the tank from the air stone.

    6. Run the line from the water pump up to the end of the growth tray that is extended higher.

    7. Run your system with both the air stone and the water pump on and the water should create a thin, film of water that flows consistently through the roots of the plants in the growth tray, and back out into the reservoir.

- Aeroponics- Again, this system can be complex and hard to assemble alone. The best idea is to get a kit from a local store and assemble from there. Here are a few links of places you can purchase something that may work for you:

    http://aeroponics.com/

CHAPTER 6

So now you either have your system up and running or you're planning where to go to get your startup kit. Many often see hydroponics as a fun and educational tool, but it really is so much more. In this final chapter I'd like to explore the benefits of using hydroponics so that you can create goals that you can set for your garden. The benefits are abundant, but here are the most common ones.

There is no soil! This is a definite advantage. You may find yourself in a situation where the typical way of planting vegetables isn't an option. Perhaps you live in an apartment but you want to grow fresh vegetables in a new way, try your hand at hydroponics. No one wants to carry bags of messy soil up to the apartment and this is a cleaner way to creating a thriving garden.

Save money on water! Since the water in many of these systems is reused and is also confined you save the cost of running water over and over again to water your garden. How often have you spent time outside arranging the sprinklers so that everything in the garden gets wet? Using a hydroponic system can help fix that problem,

Production is reliable! You can use hydroponics with ease and once the ball is rolling you have learned the tricks that will ensure you will have the same results again next time. Since your plants are not planted in the ground you don't have to worry about frost or conditions that could affect the outcome of your product.

Its portability! So you want to move your garden onto your porch? Now you can do that easily since your garden is portable. Not only can this be a wonderful thing to make life easier on you, but it also keeps pests and bugs away from your plants. You can have a hand in keeping your plants healthy and happy this way.

Year round growth potential! There is no need to plant with the change in seasons. When you use hydroponics you can use the indoor as a nesting place for your plants when necessary. You're not at the mercy of the weather - you're in control.

No more weeding! I think this may be my favorite one. When you use hydroponics you eliminate the weeding process. No pesky weeds popping up and creating a day-long event where you are on your hands and knees in a garden or lugging around the tiller to keep your plants happy. When you have a controlled sizeable area, you keep things going smoothly and less maintenance is required.

More and more again! Studies have shown that plants grown in a hydroponic environment are always better in flavor and nutritional value and will yield more. Your ability to grow two or three times the volume makes the hydroponic garden a successful one. It can be noted that your plants can grow 30-50 percent faster than soil based plants.

We can change the way we grow and in turn change the world! We wake up every morning and head out to start the day, not giving any thought to the ground beneath our feet. There are so many countries that do not have the luxury of having soil, rich in nutrients that will allow them to plant foods to help them survive. Hydroponics is a solution for all of the places that are seeking alternate solutions to growing food. When we eliminate the need for soil, we are opening doors for others who may need hydroponics to survive.

CONCLUSION

So what happens now? You have the tools here to create your only hydroponic system and not only create a wonderful bounty of veggies and herbs, but you have a better understanding of nutrients as well as pH. You can have a one pot garden or a massive undertaking, but whatever you decide, I hope you enjoy and appreciate the hydroponic way of growing. There are a number of kits that you can purchase online as well as all of the materials you will need to get your garden growing.

If you want to use things around your house, or buy a kit the results will be the same as long as you put your hard work and new knowledge into it. Like anything else worth having, a flourishing garden relies on a smart system and consistent effort.

Good luck and happy growing!

Finally, if you enjoyed this book, please take the time to share your thoughts and post a review on Amazon. It'd be greatly appreciated!

Thank you and good luck!

Preview: The Hydroponic Garden: A Start Up Guide To A Flourishing And Abundant Hydroponic Yield

Edible and Medicinal Succulents

Not only do succulents offer a wide variety of options for the beautification of your garden, many of them have practical purposes, as well. The act of growing succulents can feed our souls, and we can nourish and heal our bodies with their byproducts.

Edible cacti

For instance, one of the most common edible succulents is the prickly pear, a member of the Opuntia species. You can find their flat, paddle-like leaves and pink, oval fruit (referred to as "tunas") in specialty food markets, de-thorned and ready to be consumed. Due to their rich flavor, many call this plant 'Indian fig', and it is used in cooking and creating delicious dishes in the southwest U.S. as well as Central America.

The organ pipe cactus (Stenocereus thurberi) also bears an edible fruit, red in color and called pitahaya dulce, as well as lavendar flowers.

The barrel cactus is one of the easiest to eat, as it has no spines. This succulent can be eaten raw, and not only is its flesh edible, so are its buds and flowers.

Hylocereus, or the dragon fruit cactus, is a night bloomer that sprouts aromatic white flowers, long fleshy leaves and red or yellow fruit with crunchy seeds at the center. This plant has a high nutritional content.

Edible succulents

The agave plant, with its wide, thin leaves is used to make tequila and as a sweetener in syrups, nectars, and candy, to name a few.

All of the sedum species are edible and are generally used in salads, offering a peppery sour taste.

And while purslane is considered a weed in the U.S., it is said to be one of the more tasty succulents when fried, tossed in salads, or cooked in stews.[28]

Aloe vera is mostly known for its ability to sooth burns, and its sap is also sold and consumed in liquid form as a digestive remedy. Due to its somewhat bitter taste, most people prefer to mix the aloe juice with other liquids and foods, such as in smoothies, to mask the taste.

Mission lettuce is an under-recognized succulent that can be eaten raw or cooked. Many prefer the latter, which brings out a sweetness hidden in the plant, while the raw version causes some to experience a chalky taste.

And then there's the yucca plant, one of the most versatile of all succulents. Most parts of this plant, including the stems, fruit, and seeds, can be eaten, and they all hold high nutritional value. The leaves can also be enjoyed, steamed or sautéed; however, it's best to avoid the root, as it has a soapy taste and has been known to give some who ingest it stomach problems.[29]

Medicinal cacti

In addition to the cactus family's level of edibility, it is believed by many to have healing properties, as well.

For example, the juice from the San Pedro cactus is believed to prevent bladder and kidney issues and to treat hepatitis and high fevers.

Hoodia is believed to help suppress appetite and, therefore, effectually treat obesity.

And due to the propensity of flavanoids in the prickly pear, some believe this plant could potentially be a game-changer in terms of its detoxifying effect on the body, thus giving it the ability to prevent damage to cells and aid issues around health problems related to aging, as well as cancer. Recognizing its abundant health properties, health food stores and natural food companies offer cleaned and de-thorned prickly pear pads for consumption along with recipes.[30]

Medicinal succulents

Just as with cacti, succulents outside the cactus family also hold medicinal qualities.

For instance, in addition to Aloe's (also called Cape aloe or bitter aloe) ability to heal topically when applied to skin scrapes and burns, it is also used in lotions and can be applied directly to the skin when mixed with oils as a skin rejuvenator. Aloe is can also be taken internally as a laxative and for stomach upset. Its sap is believed to ease conjunctivitis and sinusitis.

Mostly used in Northern Africa and Europe, Boabab, or cream of tarter, is used to treat a number of ails, including fever, diarrhea, and hiccups. It is also used as an anti-inflammatory and an astringent.

The juice of the sour fig leaf is used to treat throat, oral, and fungal infections. It is used externally for burns, scrapes, and skin conditions such as eczema and internally for digestive problems and as a diuretic. It can also be used to treat toothaches, earaches, and thrush.

The fleshy leaf of the pig's ear can be used to soften and remove corns and warts. Ingested, it will cure intestinal worms, and a little leaf juice will cure toothaches and earaches. Make a hot poultice with the plant for inflammation and boils.[31]

These are a mere few examples of the diverse, practical, and beneficial uses of succulents.

Whether you purchase succulents to create a new dish or to cure a physical discomfort, you can be sure those purchased in specialty and health food markets are safe, but as with all plants growing in the wild, beware of consuming them unless you're absolutely certain of the plant's genus. When unsure, seek an expert for advice.

And as with all attempts to treat your own ailments, it's always best to consult your physician before attempting a new treatment, especially one that has not passed approval by your physician or the FDA.

As you are probably beginning to see, succulents are a multi-dimensional species, both in their form and function, and if you're a gardener who likes to not only grow plants to add beauty to your surroundings, but who endeavors to put your plants to practical use, this is another reason why succulents are a fabulous choice for you.

Click here to check out the rest of The Hydroponic Garden: A Start Up Guide To A Flourishing And Abundant Hydroponic Yield on Amazon

If the links do not work, for whatever reason, you can simply search for the pen name of the author or the name of the titles on the Amazon website to find them.

Check Out Other Better Gardening Guides Books

Below you'll find some of our other popular books that are popular on Amazon and Kindle as well. Simply click on the links below to check them out. Alternatively, you can visit our Author page on Amazon to see other work done.

Mini Farming: How to Create a Sustainable Organic Garden in Your Backyard You Can Be Proud Of

Succulent Gardening: The Beginner's Guide To Succulent Container Gardens

If the links do not work, for whatever reason, you can simply search for these titles on the Amazon website to find them.

www.ingramcontent.com/pod-product-compliance
Lightning Source LLC
Chambersburg PA
CBHW071353310526
45790CB00018B/1434